The UPSIDE-DOWN Book of SLOTHS

Elizabeth Shreeve

illustrated by
Isabella Grott

Norton Young Readers
An Imprint of W. W. Norton & Company
Celebrating a Century of Independent Publishing

For Ken—and the howler monkeys

—E. S.

I dedicate this book to those who know how to take life slowly.
It is precisely in the slow passage of time that the really important
things are perceived.

—I. G.

For information about permission to reproduce selections from this book, write to
Permissions, W. W. Norton & Company, Inc., 500 Fifth Avenue, New York, NY 10110

For information about special discounts for bulk purchases, please contact
W. W. Norton Special Sales at specialsales@wwnorton.com or 800-233-4830

Manufacturing by RRD Asia
Book design by Hana Anouk Nakamura
Production manager: Delaney Adams

ISBN 978-1-324-01577-2

W. W. Norton & Company, Inc., 500 Fifth Avenue, New York, N.Y. 10110
www.wwnorton.com

W. W. Norton & Company Ltd., 15 Carlisle Street, London W1D 3BS

1 2 3 4 5 6 7 8 9 0

SLOTHS

Slow.

Sleepy.

Weirdly adorable.

If you love sloths, you might know that there are six different types, all hanging out in the treetops of Central and South America. But did you know that there used to be dozens of others— amazing, enormous, and unlike any other animals in our world?

Well, hold on tight to that branch.

Because everything you thought about sloths is about to turn . . .

. . . upside down!

Hoffman's sloth (two-toed)

Pale-throated sloth (three-toed)

Maned sloth (three toed)

Three-toed sloths have three "fingers," or *digits*, on each of their front feet. They have small, round heads, bandit-like masks, and peaceful smiles.

Two-toed sloths—yup, you guessed it: two digits on each front foot!—are larger and more active, with piglike snouts and long brown or blond hair. Both groups have three toes on their back feet.

SiX SLOTHS IN A TREE

Today, the family tree of sloths includes six different species. They are all called *tree sloths* because they live in trees, where they hang upside down by their claws. They share a common ancestor with prehistoric *ground sloths*, which were generally much bigger and lived with their feet set firmly on land.

So how did all modern-day sloths end up topsy-turvy in the leaves? To find out, we need to look back in time—way back, over millions of years—and compare tree sloths with some of their ground sloth relatives from long ago.

Pygmy sloth (three-toed)

Brown-throated sloth (three-toed)

Linnaeus's sloth (two-toed)

SMALL

The tree sloths of our world are small and lightweight. This enables them to climb, feed, and hang among the upper branches of tropical forests.

The largest tree sloths reach a length of 32 inches, about as long as a standard poodle. They weigh a maximum of 24 pounds—and that's with a belly full of leaves. The pygmy sloth, tiniest of all, weighs no more than 7 pounds. That's the size of a slightly chubby Chihuahua.

But long ago . . .

Pygmy Sloth (*Bradypus pygmaeus*)

Pygmy sloths live on Escudo de Veraguas, a tiny remote island off the shore of Panama. They feed mostly on the leaves of red mangrove trees along the shorelines but sometimes make leisurely jaunts into the island's inland forests.

These sloths are about half the size of their closest relatives on the mainland. This is due to a process called *insular dwarfism*. When animals are limited to a small area, such as an island, their food sources shrink. This favors smaller individuals that don't need as much food to survive and produce offspring. Over many generations, the average size of animals within the population decreases.

RANGE: Isla Escudo de Veraguas, Republic of Panama

MAXIMUM SIZE: 20 inches long; 7 pounds

STATUS: Critically Endangered

Megatherium

Megatherium was the first giant ground sloth to be discovered, back in 1788. This was 30 years before large dinosaur fossils came to the attention of scientists. No one had ever seen anything so strange and immense.

Could it be a bear? An elephant? An overgrown ape?

The mysterious skeleton was shipped from Argentina to Spain, where it became part of the king's cabinet of curiosities and the first fossil of any animal to be exhibited in a lifelike position. It soon caught the attention of French scientist Georges Cuvier, who compared its claws to those of smaller sloths living in tropical forests of South America. This, he declared, was a giant sloth—a creature from the distant past.

Based on fossilized footprints, scientists estimate that *Megatherium* could lumber along on all fours at about 350 feet per minute, or 4 miles per hour (that's the speed of a fast-walking person). Thick, muscular tails enabled them to balance on their hind legs to reach food or fend off predators with their sharp front claws.

After all, *Megatherium* was 20 times the size of a saber-toothed cat!

Megatherium *claw*
(eight inches)

Tree sloth claw
(3 to 4 inches)

RANGE: South America, primarily woodlands and grasslands
MAXIMUM SIZE: 18 feet tall; 8,000 pounds
TIME PERIOD: 5 million years ago to 10,000 years ago
NAME MEANS: "Giant Beast"

HUGE

Prehistoric sloths were huge!

The earliest sloths originated in South America some 40 million years ago. Starting around 10 million years ago, some of them evolved into enormous animals called *giant ground sloths*. The ground sloth we call *Megatherium* was as big as today's elephants. It grew to 18 feet long and typically weighed about 8,000 pounds.

That's heavier than a thousand pygmy sloths!

Giant ground sloths were much too big to climb trees like the sloths of today. Instead, they reared up on their massive hind legs to rip bark from trunks and pull entire branches down with their long, curved claws.

Crack, snap . . . CRASH!

Prehistoric Connections

Around three million years ago, a land bridge finished forming between North and South America. This made it easier for animals to migrate between continents in an event known as the Great American Biotic Interchange. Carnivores like cougars, wolves, and bears moved southward, as did several types of hooved animals, like tapirs, deer, and horses. Ground sloths migrated northward along with other South American animals, some of which evolved into modern-day armadillos, porcupines, and opossums.

This was not, however, the first time that ground sloths had arrived in North America. Nine million years ago, different types of sloths made the trip by island-hopping across the seaway that separated the continents. Fossils found on Caribbean islands suggest that other sloths traveled from South America to the West Indies even earlier, around 33 million years ago.

Ancient Cousins

How do we know which animals are related?

Scientists start with fossilized bones, which reveal how prehistoric creatures looked and moved. They link fossils to time periods to understand how features like hip joints or skulls were passed down over time. Molecular data, such as DNA, can reveal even more.

From methods like these, we know that sloths, anteaters, and armadillos are all part of a group known as *xenarthrans*, meaning "strange joint." All xenarthrans have extra connections in their backbones that strengthen the animal's front legs for digging, which is how anteaters and armadillos obtain food.

Some 60 million years ago, soon after the dinosaur era, the earliest xenarthrans of South America began evolving into a rich array of animals— plant-munching sloths, insect-slurping anteaters, and their distant relatives, the armadillos and now-extinct glyptodonts.

Ice Age Giants

Giant ground sloths were one of the humongous creatures known as the *Ice Age megafauna*. In the Americas, these included woolly mammoths, dire wolves, saber-toothed cats, and car-sized relatives of armadillos called *glyptodonts*.

These super-sized creatures disappeared around 10,000 years ago. Experts aren't sure why. Some point to the changes caused by a warming climate, an increase in hunting by humans, or a combination of impacts. This is a mystery that's yet to be solved—perhaps by someone like you!

TREE HUGGERS

Tree sloths hate to travel.

These days, all sloths live in small areas of tropical rainforests in Central and South America. They hide in the tree canopy and come down to the ground only once a week—to poop.

Yup, that's right. Once a week, sloths shinny down tree trunks, dig holes using their short tails, and do their business. Finally, mission accomplished, they climb back up and settle in for another quiet week of tree-hugging, leaf-munching, and napping.

But sloths weren't always such homebodies.

Long ago . . .

Brown-Throated Sloth (*Bradypus variegatus*)

Brown-throated sloths are the most common tree sloths. They live in a variety of forest habitats from Central America to the middle of South America.

These sloths have strong, short tails and arms that are twice as long as their legs. Their facial markings give them permanent smiles, but that doesn't mean they're always happy or peaceful. In fact, males will defend their territory by swinging their sharp claws at each other in super-slow-motion boxing matches.

Like other sloths, brown-throated sloths sometimes look green because tiny, plantlike life-forms called *algae* grow on their fur. This helps the animals blend into the forest. In exchange, the algae find shelter and water within tiny grooves in the sloths' long, coarse hairs.

RANGE: Honduras, Central America to Peru and Bolivia, South America

MAXIMUM SIZE: 27 inches long; 14 pounds

STATUS: Least Concern

Eremotherium

The tallest of all prehistoric ground sloths, *Eremotherium* also had the widest geographic range. Its fossils have been found in locations from Brazil, Peru, Ecuador, and Central America all the way north to Texas, Florida, South Carolina, and New Jersey.

Eremotherium and other giant ground sloths moved north during *interglacial* periods when the climate warmed. From studying chemicals in its teeth, we also know that *Eremotherium* adapted to a range of wet and dry conditions by changing its diet. This helped it survive difficult conditions, such as cooler temperatures during the peak of the Ice Age. *Eremotherium* was tough!

RANGE: Northern Atlantic coast of the United States to southern Brazil

MAXIMUM SIZE: 20 feet tall; 7,000 pounds

TIME PERIOD: 4.9 million years ago to 11,000 years ago

NAME MEANS: "Solitary Beast"

EXPLORERS

Ground sloths once traveled all over the Americas!

If you live anywhere between Canada and southern Chile, it's possible that a prehistoric sloth once lived there, too. During a period of warmer weather, one type of sloth ranged as far north as Alaska. Other sloths reached the Caribbean islands by swimming between islands and walking across what was then dry land.

To survive in these different areas, prehistoric sloths adapted to a wide variety of habitats and lifestyles. And if conditions changed and food got scarce, they sometimes left familiar territory and set off to find new homes.

How Sleepy and Slow Is a Sloth?

If you think of tree sloths as the superstars of snooze . . . think again.

Sure, it's true that sloths in captivity spend most of their time asleep. But scientists have discovered that wild sloths sleep only about 10 hours per day, usually curled up in comfy trees or hanging from branches. (Compare this to koalas, the true champions of naptime, who slumber twice that much.)

Sloths definitely win the prize, however, as the slowest mammals. They move through trees at a pace of about 13 feet per minute, much slower than other easygoing mammals like those drowsy koalas. On the ground, sloths crawl even more slowly, dragging themselves along the forest floor with their arms at only about one foot per minute. In comparison, the average walking speed for a person is 270 feet per minute. When they drop from the trees into water, however . . .

It's a Swim Race!

Believe it or not, tree sloths are excellent swimmers. They float easily, can hold their breath for long periods, and are known to move three times faster in water than on the land.

Those extra-long necks help, too, by keeping sloths' heads above water. Most mammals have seven vertebrae, or bony rings, in their necks, but some tree sloths have nine.

This allows them to swivel their heads like owls and scan for danger without moving their entire bodies.

Maybe that's why a sloth's smile always seems to be right side up!

SHY LONERS

Tree sloths live quiet lives.

Their slow habits keep them hidden from predators like jaguars, ocelots, and their worst enemy of all, the harpy eagle, famous for its 7-foot wingspan and talons larger than a grizzly bear's claws. These powerful hunters detect prey by scanning for quick movements, but sloths don't move much faster than the leaves around them. When startled, they freeze in place. Their predators don't even see them!

Tree sloths are usually alone, too. This makes them even more difficult to spot. Other than mothers with babies, you won't often find more than one sloth in a single tree.

But long ago . . .

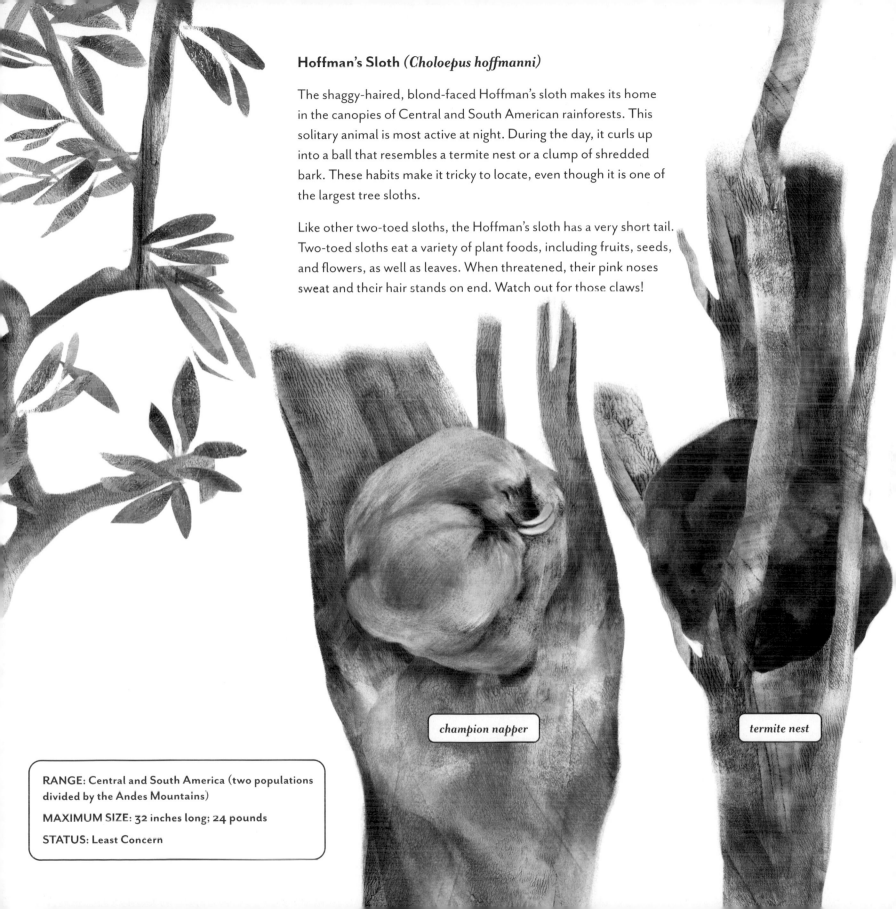

Hoffman's Sloth (*Choloepus hoffmanni*)

The shaggy-haired, blond-faced Hoffman's sloth makes its home in the canopies of Central and South American rainforests. This solitary animal is most active at night. During the day, it curls up into a ball that resembles a termite nest or a clump of shredded bark. These habits make it tricky to locate, even though it is one of the largest tree sloths.

Like other two-toed sloths, the Hoffman's sloth has a very short tail. Two-toed sloths eat a variety of plant foods, including fruits, seeds, and flowers, as well as leaves. When threatened, their pink noses sweat and their hair stands on end. Watch out for those claws!

champion napper

termite nest

RANGE: Central and South America (two populations divided by the Andes Mountains)

MAXIMUM SIZE: 32 inches long; 24 pounds

STATUS: Least Concern

Harlan's Ground Sloth (*Paramylodon*)

This medium-sized ground sloth inhabited the grasslands of North America, where it grazed alongside mammoths, bison, and horses. Predators like saber-toothed cats, dire wolves, and lions hunted these herbivores. *Paramylodon* defended itself with strong claws, stout limbs, and thick, armor-like skin embedded with small, pebble-like bones called *osteoderms*. The fossils of *Paramylodon* and some other ground sloths suggest that they had long, powerful prehensile tongues for snapping up the best leaves, similar to giraffes of today.

In the 1880s, a set of unusual fossilized footprints was discovered near the Nevada State Prison. Authorities announced that the prints must be those of a giant human—walking in sandals! We now know that the tracks were left by *Paramylodon*, which walked on the sides of its feet with its long claws curled inward. Other ground sloths shared this trait, which probably caused them to waddle as they left those puzzling footprints behind.

Paramylodon

RANGE: North America, from Washington State south to southern Mexico

MAXIMUM SIZE: 10 feet long; 2,400 pounds

TIME PERIOD: 2.5 million years ago to 12,000 years ago

NAME MEANS: "Related to Mill-Tooth"

TOUGH HERDS

Some ground sloths lived in herds, like hippos.

In Ecuador, scientists found fossils of a group of giant sloths, including approximately twenty-two adults and young. The discovery suggests that, around 20,000 years ago, the herd was grazing together when their watering hole dried up and left them stranded.

Other discoveries reveal that prehistoric ground sloths were well-equipped to defend themselves from enemies. Many had long, sharp claws. Others appear to have dug huge burrows, leaving behind tunnels that stretch for hundreds of feet into rocky hillsides. Today, we find their massive claw marks on the tunnel walls.

But what was one thing those tough prehistoric giants couldn't do?

Hang upside down in the treetops!

It's an Upside-Down Life

When you hang upside down, your face turns red. Your vision blurs. Your lungs feel squished. And if you're trying to hold on by your feet—well, forget it.

How do sloths do it?

Over many thousands of years, tree sloths have gradually adapted to upside-down life. Their claws have a tough core of bone covered with a layer of *keratin*, the same flexible material that makes up our fingernails and hair. These curved claws act like hooks that automatically close when they're resting. Sometimes dead sloths are found still clamped to branches.

Tree sloths are strong, too. They have one third less muscle mass than animals of similar size, but their specialized muscle fibers provide loads of endurance. Inside their bodies, small skin tabs connect internal organs to ribs. This prevents their heavy, leaf-filled stomachs from pressing down on their lungs. And check out the crazy hairstyles! Unlike other mammals, the hair of tree sloths grows up and backwards from the stomach. During a tropical rainstorm, this helps water drain quickly off those furry, upside-down bodies.

All this means that tree sloths can eat, sleep, mate, and give birth while suspended blissfully among the leaves. And speaking of babies . . .

Sloth Families

A baby sloth enters the world with open eyes, sharp claws, and a full coat of fur. After feeding on its mother's milk for a month, it begins to sample leaves from her mouth and learns what plants to eat. At about six months old, the young sloth leaves mom's protective hug to explore nearby branches. They gradually drift apart until the mother sloth moves away, sometimes to a nearby or overlapping area.

After babyhood, a wild sloth lives a solitary life. So how does it find a mate? Female three-toed sloths solve this problem . . . by screaming! Their high-pitched calls attract males, who sometimes fight each other in a contest for sloth romance before the two mates go their separate ways again.

LEAF-MUNCHERS

Tree sloths eat leaves, which don't provide much nutrition. And they eat much less than other leaf-eating animals of the rainforest.

How do they survive?

The secret lies in their supremely slow habits. Instead of gobbling food all day like a noisy, acrobatic monkey, a tree sloth simply . . . does less. It stays quiet. It barely moves. Once in a while, it reaches for some nearby foliage to nibble. Even its digestion works slowly. Humans digest food in a few days, but a sloth's meal takes over a month to make it through.

Munch . . . munch . . . munch.

For tree sloths, leaves are on the menu for every meal.

But long ago . . .

Maned Sloth (*Bradypus torquatus*)

Maned sloths occupy two strips of coastal forest in eastern Brazil. Named for the circle of dark hair around the necks of adult males, these sloths rarely descend from the canopy and cannot stand or walk on the ground. Northern and southern populations have been separated for over four million years and may be diverging into two separate species.

Like other three-toed sloths, maned sloths feed on the leaves of a few forest trees, especially those of the Cecropia. Their slow digestion means that they can eat plants that would be toxic to other animals. As they chew on plants, their soft teeth wear down and regrow. Scientists have compared their teeth to the fossilized teeth of prehistoric sloths in order to understand each animal's diet, lifestyle, and ecosystem.

RANGE: Patches of coastal Brazilian Atlantic rainforest
MAXIMUM SIZE: 30 inches long; 20 pounds
STATUS: Vulnerable to Extinction

Thalassocnus

Fossils of this unique group of sloths tell the story of a gradual transition to life in the ocean. The earliest *Thalassocnus* probably waded in shallow waters to graze on sea grasses and other marine plants. Later *Thalassocnus* may have pulled themselves along the seafloor with their claws. Fossils of their broken bones suggest that they braved some rough waves in the quest to survive. Other *Thalassocnus* fossils show the teeth marks of sharks that preyed on them. The ocean was a dangerous place!

Over time, *Thalassocnus* developed special body features for swimming. Their bones became denser, allowing them to dive like manatees. Their nostrils moved higher on their heads, like those of crocodiles or hippos, so they could breathe while partly submerged. Their long tails helped them balance, like beavers. Some grew larger than today's sea lions. Today, we find their fossils alongside those of other aquatic animals like whales, sharks, and crocodiles.

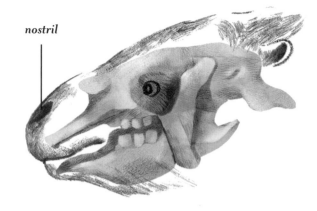

nostril

Thalassocnus *skull view*

RANGE: Pacific coast of Peru and Chile

MAXIMUM SIZE: 9 feet long (including tail); 200 pounds

TIME PERIOD: 8 million to 3 million years ago

NAME MEANS: "Lazy One of the Sea"

OCEAN FORAGERS

Ground sloths of old ate all kinds of plants.

As they roamed the Americas, ground sloths adapted to eating a variety of vegetation, from prickly cactus to fruits, bark, and leaves. Different sloths ate different foods, too. This allowed multiple types of ground sloths to live side by side without competing with each other.

Around eight million years ago, the Pacific coast of South America grew dry and hot. To adapt to these conditions, one group of ground sloths, *Thalassocnus*, did something that no other sloths had ever done—they took to the ocean and began foraging for sea grasses.

Imagine a rocky beach, sparkling waves . . . and a body-surfing sloth!

Secrets of Sloth Poop

Why do sloths come down to the
forest floor to poop?

The tree sloths may be marking territory or
advertising for a mate. Another answer lies in the
relationship between sloths and a type of moth that lives in their
fur. When a tree sloth poops on the ground, female moths hop
off to lay eggs. The larvae feed on the dung. When they hatch into
adult moths, they fly up to nestle safely into a sloth's fur again.
Researchers have used special vacuum cleaners to remove bugs from
a sloth's coat—and found more than 150 moths on a single animal.

Yikes! Sounds itchy. So what's the benefit to sloths? Scientists
believe that moths provide nutrients that help algae grow in the
sloths' fur. This keeps the animals camouflaged against possible
predators. Sloths may also feed on the algae as a snack.

It's a sloth-moth love fest!

Moth larva

Adult sloth moth

Mystery of the Long Fur Coat

Like other mammals, people are warm-blooded. This means that our bodies generate heat by converting food into energy. If temperatures fall, we start to shiver.

Not sloths. Even though tree sloths are warm-blooded, their bodies maintain a lower temperature than humans could withstand—a helpful adaptation for surviving on a low-calorie diet of leaves. And their muscles, so perfect for slow-motion endurance, can't manage the rapid movement of shivering. Instead, they grow long fur coats that seem out of place in a tropical rainforest. On cool mornings, they climb to the tip-tops of trees to bask in the sun, like snakes or other cold-blooded creatures. As the day heats up, they slowly make their way back to the shade.

ADORABLE

It's hard to imagine anything cuter than
a peaceful, smiling sloth. Except . . . how
about a whole bunch of baby sloths, piled in
a heap?

At sloth sanctuaries, orphaned babies
snuggle with stuffed toys. They take leisurely,
upside-down strolls across miniature jungle
gyms. They reach out their long, skinny
arms like they want to be held. Visitors are
not allowed to touch them—that could be
harmful to the animals—but it's hard to
resist.

These wonderful creatures are
hardwired for hugging. In the wild,
this guarantees that babies stay safe in
their mothers' arms when they're way
up high in a tree. And did I mention that
they're really, really cute?

But long, long ago . . .

Pale-Throated Sloth (*Bradypus tridactylus*)

The pale-throated sloth is sometimes called the *ai* because of its birdlike whistle. Like other three-toed sloths, its wiry, blackish-gray fur helps it blend in against the rough bark of trees.

These tree sloths have pale-yellow patches of fur on their throats. The males develop an orange, yellow, and white patch on their backs, called a *speculum*. Pygmy and brown-throated sloths also grow these patches, which secrete a musty-smelling oil. With bright colors and strong scents, the males are telling their sloth neighbors, *Hey, this is my territory!*

RANGE: Northern parts of South America from French Guiana to Suriname and Venezuela

MAXIMUM SIZE: 27 inches long; 14 pounds

STATUS: Least Concern

Hapalops

Long before giant ground sloths like *Megatherium* emerged during the Ice Age, most sloths were moderate or small in size. *Hapalops*, one of the earlier sloths to leave behind complete skeletons, was lightweight enough to climb trees and walk along the strong lower branches. This would have helped it to avoid predators of the time, such as fierce, hook-beaked terror birds.

Much later, on the Caribbean islands, a separate branch of the sloth family tree also developed small bodies suited to climbing. The island-dweller known as *Neocnus*, or "new sloth," survived until around 4,500 years ago, a time when people were building the first pyramids in Egypt. It was the last ground sloth to go extinct.

RANGE: South America including wooded savannas of Colombia, Brazil, Bolivia, and Argentina

MAXIMUM SIZE: 3.5 feet long; 85 pounds

TIME PERIOD: 20 million to 7 million years ago

NAME MEANS: "Gentle Face"

WEiRD

Prehistoric sloths weren't all that cute.

Based on what we know from fossils, they had thick chests, muscular legs, and hefty tails. Their shoulders slumped. Their heavy feet curled inward. They would have looked like enormous, lumpy baked potatoes as they trudged across the countryside, ripping down branches and gobbling shrubs.

Sounds nothing like today's adorable tree sloths, right? But those ancient sloths had the same sorts of sharp claws and unusual teeth, joints, and bones as their modern descendants. They moved slowly and ate only plants. Some of the smaller ones may even have climbed trees.

Tracking Down Tree Sloths

How do you study an animal that's hidden in vine-clad treetops?

Sloth researchers strap on their binoculars and snake-proof boots. Some hoist themselves high into the tree canopy using special climbing equipment. When they safely capture a sloth, they check its health and gather a few hairs for DNA analysis. Other researchers attach miniature backpacks containing data loggers, GPS trackers, and tiny transmitters to sloths. These allow the scientists to relocate the sloths after they disappear into the forest again.

Deciphering Fossils

Scientists figure out the diets of prehistoric sloths by studying fossilized teeth, jaws, and other body parts. And one more thing—poop.

In dry caves within Arizona's Grand Canyon, Shasta ground sloths left behind a plentiful supply of fossil dung, called *coprolite*, alongside their skeletons. Scientists have also found a few extremely rare specimens of mummified hair and skin. From these ancient remains, we know that the bear-sized animals ate a wide range of plants, including cactus, yucca, agave, acacia, juniper, Joshua trees, and grasses. They ate plants that modern animals won't nibble, like creosote and saltbush. Coprolites even tell us what types of parasites may have caused giant ground sloth stomachaches!

Presidential Sloth

Thomas Jefferson, the third US president, loved to collect fossils. In 1796, a friend sent him fossils of an enormous sloth from what is now West Virginia. In his excitement, Jefferson initially compared the animal's claws to those of an enormous lion. He named it *Megalonyx*, meaning "giant claw."

Jefferson soon realized that the animal was related to the giant ground sloths of South America. He believed, however, that *Megalonyx* was still roaming the wilderness. He even encouraged the explorers Lewis and Clark to be on the lookout during their westward journey. Surely the vast, uncharted continent must contain the world's largest and most fearsome animals!

President Jefferson's enthusiasm for *Megalonyx* helped to initiate the study of fossils and paleontology in North America, leading to discoveries of dinosaurs and other prehistoric life across the continent.

A World for Sloths

Today some tree sloth populations are stable, while others—pygmy sloths and maned sloths—are critically endangered. One threat is the illegal pet trade. Because of their popularity, sloths are often taken from the wild and sold. A majority are babies that are stolen from their mothers. Many die during transport or when they are given the wrong food.

Another major threat is loss of habitat. Unlike their prehistoric ancestors, tree sloths can't easily move to new places or adjust to rapid changes in the environment. They belong to the rainforest, as a vital part of the ecosystem.

SLACKERS?

Sure, they're slow. They're skinny, scraggly haired, covered with algae, and crawling with moths. They have lousy eyesight, and when they fall or climb down from a tree, they are nearly helpless on the ground. It's not surprising that early explorers named them for one of the seven deadly sins—*sloth*, meaning "laziness."

Yet tree sloths are part of our world today, long after their bigger, tougher ancestors went extinct. So maybe they aren't slackers . . .

Linnaeus's Sloth (*Choloepus didactylus*)

This two-toed sloth inhabits the wet tropical forests of northern South America. Like its close cousin the Hoffman's sloth, this normally gentle sloth will hiss, bite, and slash with its foreclaws when threatened. If confronted with a predator while on the ground, it rears up on its hind legs and tries to run backward—sometimes crashing into trees by mistake.

RANGE: Northern areas of South America including Venezuela, Colombia, Ecuador, Peru, northern Brazil, and the Guianas

MAXIMUM SIZE: 32 inches; 24 pounds

STATUS: Least Concern

SURVIVORS

Tree sloths are survivors.

Masters of camouflage. Experts in energy efficiency.

By slowing down, tree sloths have carved out a special niche. They consume less food. They eat plants that other animals avoid. Instead of running or jumping or making lots of noise, they disappear into a slow-motion time zone that's all their own.

Over the last 40 million years, sloths have roamed the Americas, defended against giant predators, and surfed the sea. Today, the rainforest canopy is their highway and their home. All they need is a healthy rainforest and a quiet life in the trees.

And now . . .

. . . it's time for a sloth slumber party!

TIMELINE OF SLOTH HISTORY

mya = million years ago
ya = years ago

Today: Six species of tree sloths live in Central and South America

1831–1836: Charles Darwin finds ground sloth fossils in South America

1797: First ground sloth fossil identified in US; Thomas Jefferson names it *Megalonyx*

1788: *Megatherium* fossil discovered in Argentina

4,500 ya: Ground sloths disappear from Caribbean islands

10,000 ya: Ground sloths extinct in North, Central, and South America

40,000 to 10,000 ya: Ground sloths trapped in La Brea Tar Pits (Los Angeles)

125,000 to 75,000 ya: *Megalonyx* reaches Alaska and the Yukon

2.5 mya to 12,000 ya: *Paramylodon* lives in North America

3 mya: More ground sloths migrate to North America during Great American Biotic Interchange

5 mya to 10,000 ya: Giant ground sloths inhabit North, Central, and South America

8 mya to 3 mya: *Thalassocnus* lives along Pacific coast of South America

9 mya: First ground sloths migrate to North America

20 mya to 7 mya: *Hapalops* lives in South America

25 to 5 mya: Ground sloths diversify into many new groups and species

27 mya: Last common ancestor of two-toed and three-toed tree sloths

33 mya: Some ground sloths migrate to Caribbean islands

50 mya: Early evidence of ground sloth ancestors

60 to 66 mya: Xenarthrans (armadillos, anteaters, and sloths) emerge in South America; the Pilosa (sloths and anteaters) split from the Cingulata (armadillos)

66 mya: Dinosaur extinction; Age of Mammals begins

AUTHOR'S NOTE

Sloths cast magical spells. I am deeply indebted to the experts whose research and publications helped me understand their lives and origins. In particular, Dr. Greg McDonald (Bureau of Land Management, retired), Dr. Mariella Superina (IUCN/SSC Anteater, Sloth and Armadillo Specialist Group), and Dr. Donald Grayson (University of Washington) have guided this book through many drafts. Dr. Emily Lindsey (La Brea Tar Pits and Museum) and Dr. Ross MacPhee (American Museum of Natural History) generously reviewed early versions. At the Smithsonian National Museum of Natural History, curator Dave Bohaska provided an unforgettable tour of the collections, igniting a lifelong fascination with fossilized poop. Thanks also to the Sloth Conservation Foundation for the reference image of a backpack-wearing sloth.

Heartfelt appreciation to my agent, Ammi-Joan Paquette, and editor, Simon Boughton, for cheering and steering the book. Huge thanks to Isabella Grott for beautiful artwork that brought words to life and to Hana Anouk Nakamura and others at Norton Young Readers for creative design and production. As always, I am grateful for writing comrades, especially Alexandria Giardino, Amanda Conran, Darcey Rosenblatt, Heather Montgomery, and Laurie Thompson. Giant ground sloth–sized hugs to my husband, Ken, and our kids for enduring months of sloth trivia and questionable jokes involving coprolite.

Note on Toes:

Some sloth experts refer to digits of sloth forelimbs as "fingers." I've chosen to use "toes" in reference to all digits, consistent with terminology used by the International Union for Conservation of Nature (IUCN).

LEARN MORE

The Adventures of Dr. Sloth: Rebecca Cliffe and Her Quest to Protect Sloths, by Suzi Eszterhas. Millbrook Press, 2022.

Mega Meltdown: The Weird and Wonderful Animals of the Ice Age, by Jack Tite. Blueprint Editions, 2018.

PBS *Eons* video: "How Sloths Went from the Seas to the Trees." Available on YouTube or at **PBS.org**.

American Museum of Natural History: **www.amnh.org**

La Brea Tar Pits & Museum: **www.tarpits.org**

The Sloth Institute: **www.theslothinstitute.org**

The Sloth Conservation Foundation: **www.slothconservation.com**

Kids Saving the Rainforest: **www.kidssavingtherainforest.org**

IUCN/SSC Anteater, Sloth and Armadillo Specialist Group: **www.xenarthrans.org**

For more learning, teaching, and conservation resources, please visit **www.elizabethshreeve.com**.